From Ours To Yours

Eleni Sophia & pn.writes

Copyright © 2020 Eleni Sophia & pn.writes

'From Ours to Yours'

Perspective Press Global Ltd

All rights reserved.

ISBN: 978-1-8380044-4-6

DEDICATION

This book is from our love, to your love;
We wrote this as a token of appreciation
Our appreciation for one another
Our appreciation for you
And our appreciation for love.
To prove to you that true love does exist-
But first, first you have to fill your own cup with endless self-love
You have to be patient and trust the process

We wrote this to remind you that
Even if the distance does get tough
Even if you are from different backgrounds
Nothing should get in the way- especially if something is what you truly want
Do not ever stop fighting for your happiness
Put your happiness first
Always
And never give up on what your soul craves

This life, this journey is so special
And we want to share everything with you

This is
From Ours to Yours
Love,
Eleni Sophia & pn.writes

In a generation where old school love is being craved, what is stopping us from bringing it back? In a world where loyalty is perceived a luxury, what is stopping us from normalizing faithfulness?

In a generation where we are so consumed by the power of our phones, social media and who's liked who's picture,
Let us take a step back
Let us step away from our insecurities
From our egos
Let us feed each other's minds with nothing but our gratitude for one another
Let us bring back handwritten notes and letters

And it won't always be so picture perfect but that is when the power of maturity comes into the picture. We let our egos consume us to a point where we become petty and try to 'win' arguments. It is perfectly fine to acknowledge where you have gone wrong and to admit your faults;
It should never be you two against each other
Rather, you two against the situation.
Remember this.

If we want to bring back the old-school love, let us put our egos aside, let us ignite our gratitude for one another and most importantly, let us keep God/The Universe in the center.

We are so sorry if you have had a bad experience with love before;
Our aim is to show you that no matter what you have been through, when you pick
yourself up,
even with a dose of self-love and faith,

you will be absolutely fine
because one day, this love will be the epitome of the reason why the most-high didn't let you settle.
And my goodness you will be so grateful.

My darling, when you find this love that fits so elegantly,
there will be no games and
that is when you will know
the reason why God didn't allow you to settle
and this is the incredible person God had waiting for you
And it will be worth every second you waited.

Interfaith and Long-Distance, are two things the Universe thought we were both
strong enough to conquer. With trust and faith in the Universe we know we will be
guided towards the right path.
There is something up there taking care of us all and
we just need to start trusting that.

Together we aim to show you that true love does exist
In a generation where loyalty and people with pure hearts are so rare to find
We aim to show you brining back 'old school love' is still possible.

Never give up on who you love and what you believe in.
Situations can get tough but
when both of you strive and motivate one another, you will be a team.
It will never
be you two against each other;
It will be you two against the world.

And as you unravel and find your way through our journey of words, we hope you find solace.
We hope you find solace in believing everything will be okay and we hope you find solace within yourself.

We hope you enjoy our collection!

We want to show you anything is possible;
Love; the vibration of love has the highest frequency-
Nothing can ever get in the way of true love
Remember that

And one day, when we watch the kids play
When we have our own place
I cannot wait to have you by my side when we can finally
say
'we made it'

When I first met this man, I saw all the incredible potential within. No ego, so peaceful and most importantly, it was the way he treated others that sparked everything
How he balances his medical degree with everything is beyond me; he makes me so proud each day and I am so incredibly blessed to be his first love

One major thing we have in common is wanting to serve and help others; we all have a purpose in this world and I've always believed we struggle, we heal, and we create art to help the rest of the world

We wrote 'From Ours to Yours' for you. We highlight the importance of appreciation and daily gratitude for one another and we also talk about being in an interfaith and long-distance relationship. God/The Universe has a plan for us all; you cross paths with people for a reason (some people stay for a certain period and others, others are only meant to be here for a short while) however, when two people come together with strong faith and belief, you have the power to conquer anything and everything- especially if it was already written.

At the end of the day, we always *learn*. We may hurt, we heal, we find self-love, but we learn and out of this learning comes growth

And growth

Growth my darling-

It is beautiful.

Your intuition- sweetheart, your intuition is your guardian angel; it is a voice guiding you throughout life Listen.

I always knew I was meant to be a wife
That doesn't mean I was not meant to be a CEO
I was meant to be both
The right one made me realize I could be both
He made me realize there was nothing wrong with being a strong woman with ambition and being the soft caring woman, I am
Instead, he helps me achieve all my potential
And
my only intentions are to watch him manifest all his dreams and goals as I do my own

When he lets you in
Make sure to forever take care of his heart;
Our men deserve the same love we desire
Their fragility is their strength
May we learn to speak to them with kindness
May we raise them
May we elevate the King in them
And may we remind them how proud we are of everything that they do

My darling, the 'honeymoon phase' is not real
It is all in your mind
Do not let society fool you into believing a social construct.

When you have found the one who dedicates themselves to making you feel appreciated for the whole period you are theirs, it becomes clear that the honeymoon phase is nothing but a social construct.

In a society where the loss of affection in relationships is justified because of duration, let us change this and appreciate the souls and mindsets that are so rare to find- For the entire time they are ours.

Let us stop normalising the idea of loss of affection in our relationships. Let us devote this time into appreciating one another- even when things do get tough. After all, life is too short not to appreciate. Let us show our appreciation for one another daily.

After all. Life is too precious to be taken for granted. Time it too precious to be taken for granted. Love, love is too precious to be taken for granted. Let us shower our loved ones and tell them how proud we are of them. Let us tell our partners how appreciative we are of everything they do- even the little things,
After all, it is the little things that go the long way

What a lucky girl I am
To have the privilege of being your first
I pray I get to show you the beauty of love
The insights of true affection
I pray and ask for the strength and guidance to respect you exactly the way you deserve
For you give me everything;
You showed me exactly why the universe had me waiting
And I will forever be grateful to it for bringing you into my life and interlocking our wonderful paths

The way he devoured me
Made me realize how easy I was to love
What I once thought was 'love'
Is far from the definition I have now

He shows me exactly how
To be love
And to be loved

The connotations that get associated with 'home'
Comfort
Safety
Exactly how I feel when I am with you

And to live a life alongside you would be a privilege in itself
A lifetime in your arms
Your true affection
Your appreciation for women
Your respect towards women
Your acceptance for who I am in my rawest form
And your presence
Is more than anything I would have ever asked for

And when sadness lingers in his eyes
My soul misaligns
If I could physically move mountains to save him from experiencing the pain
If I could take the climb instead
Believe me I would
I pray for nothing but his happiness in this eternal life
And all other the lives to come
He deserves everything wonderful this world has to offer
And I cannot wait to watch him become the incredible man he was forever destined to be
I pray for nothing more than watching his dreams and visions manifest as I do my own

Soak yourself in an endless amount of self-love
Ask the universe for guidance
Be open to receiving
trust
And just wait until you see all the magical things you attract
But sweetheart, remember
True love cannot find you until you have found yourself first

Wonderful men still exist;
Thank you for restoring my faith in love
For loving me the way I deserve
Treating me with respect and integrity
Staying up late to help me with my businesses
Guiding me through my pitches
Being patient with me
This sure is the one in an eternity kind of love

And when you have a disagreement or when you argue
Take a moment to step back
And fully grasp how the other is feeling
Self-awareness is a beautiful trait
Especially in situations like these
For love is not a competition
Rather a team
It will never be you two against each other
But you guys against the situation-
And with this in mind,
Everything changes.
Next time you have a disagreement with your significant other- take a moment to breathe- for you never know how the other is truly feeling
Take a moment to listen
Try and comprehend
And take it from there

I was captivated by
The beauty and strength in his thoughts
The way his mind works
His mindset
His integrity
The way he treats people with so much respect
I just knew I needed this man in my life
His peace with life
His peace with everything around him
Little did he know he was my peace at the same time

We came together just as though it was written in the stars
Even before we set foot into this world
It is as though it was already written;
And our hearts came together
And our journeys intertwined
As though it was perfectly meant to be

From Ours to Yours- Eleni Sophia & pn.writes

When you let him in
Protect him dearly
He needs love just as much as you
Pray for his well-being
With your prayers, he will have everything in life and more
The purity of your prayers will protect him in everything he does
Your prayers will guard him through whatever he has to conquer
Your prayers will move mountains for this man
For our men need our words of encouragement and our elevation
Probably more than we do

Now when I lay on my side
I imagine myself on your chest
Hand on your heart
Head buried upon your skin
Hearing each breath
Seeing your chest rise up and down
Close my eyes in a moment of deep appreciation
And pray to God I never lose you

Dear Best friend,
Not being able to see you often is one of the hardest
things I face in my day to day life
But deep down, my heart knows, all of this will be worth
every moment we have had to wait
We have our entire lives ahead of us and I am so excited
to have the privilege of spending my entire life with you
Nothing hurts more than not being able to see you daily
But with love this intense
No amount of distance can ever get in the way
After all
Our love will forever outweigh the miles between us

What is home you ask?
Home is your arms around me
Your hugs from behind
Your forehead kisses-
Your random forehead kisses- even in the middle of a disagreement
for I feel nothing but peace
Heartfelt
Comfort
Home
Home is being wrapped in his arms
Yes,
that's my definition of home
you.

And sometimes I take a moment to think what a
wonderful deed I must have done to have been blessed
with a soul like yours
For, never in my life have I encountered such an entity-
-Sweetheart-
The 'dying breed' still exists
Never lose hope my darling
Your time is coming
Radiate love;
For you are love
And you will begin to attract the most wonderful
circumstances and people
-
That's it
That must have been my wonderful deed-
To have been so engulfed in self-love
And to have radiated so much love
The Universe knew we were deserving of each other

When you both come together with
Pure vibes, gratitude and good intent
Only magnificent things can start to manifest
Energy, vibes, intentions they are all so real
And when you come together and consciously spread
positivity to make the world a better place
Magical things begin to unravel

He will take his time to explore you
He will stop for a moment and gaze into your eyes
deeply
He won't rush anything
After all
All great things require patience
And all great things take time
He will take his time to explore you
He will stop for a moment and gaze into your eyes
deeply
He won't rush anything
And when you find this man
Protect his heart dearly

There is so much life has in store for us
As long as I have you by my side
I know I can accomplish it all

And when we have our disagreements, I cannot help but put myself in his position- think of the pain he is going through too
Please do not sleep on an argument- you never know the last time you may see someone
We simply cannot sleep knowing one of us is in misalignment with our love
For life is too short for our egos to get in the way of our tenderness
Let us be mature and unravel accordingly

Each rose you have ever given me
Each petal has been kept sacred
Dried in a jar
And is patiently waiting to be used as decoration on a mantlepiece
in our future living room
maybe one day the kids will ask why these petals are so special
and I cannot wait to tell them how their most amazing father gifted them to me, and how they have been cherished for all these years

And I choose you
In this life, the next live and all the lives after
I choose you;
And I will keep choosing you
It will always be you
Forever and always my handsome

What makes this so special is our mindsets, the way we think about ourselves
Love so pure even
we argue, I cannot help but think how grateful I am for the growth that will come out of this
Love and energy so strong, nobody can harm something so resilient
The appreciation we have for one another
Our bond with the divine
That's what keeps this love so sacred

Life is so incredibly short to not appreciate one another
Life is such a fragile journey and we can lose anybody anytime
Please take time out of your day to tell your loved ones how much they mean to you
In fact, take this moment to stop reading, take out your phone and either text or call somebody who means a lot to you
Tell them how much you appreciate them
And as you hear their happiness through their voice- let it engulf you
For there is nothing more amazing in this world than to spread positivity and gratitude

She was unstoppable within herself
That the universe thought she was ready to receive the love she had always desired
But first, the universe had to build her
Guide her through a journey of hurt and healing
So, she could learn what she really wanted from this world
So, she could finally see her worth
And ignite with the one who deserved her all along
And it was only then that she found him
And when she did
She finally knew what all the 'you'll see why's meant

Actions and kept promises are the catalyst to a beautiful
loving relationship
Please do not settle until you have found the love you
have forever deserved
your bravery and strength should be credited
we are so sorry if you have had a negative experience
with love
but take this moment to appreciate life
for life is so beautiful;
ask the universe for guidance
and you shall receive
you always receive

He gave my soul everything it needed
Actually, things that I didn't even know I needed
What it was always craving; he found it and fed it
He fed it with love, care and nourished it well
Without me even having to ask
Our journeys intertwined so perfectly
A time where we both had so much ahead of us
He came at exactly the right time
Going into the year
I had no idea we would meet
Just 24 days later
That's right January 24th, 2019
The day both our lives changed so unpredictably
And that, that is the purest love of them all
When everything comes together so unexpectedly
All in divine timing

And one day when love arrives
You will come to terms that love is not bad
Love does not leave you puzzled or questioning yourself
Love supports your ambitions
Love has no ego
Love does not leave you confused
Love reminds you how great you are
Day by day, love reminds you how impeccably, strong you are
Love is unimaginable
Love is teamwork
Love is not one-sided
Love is didactic
Love teaches you and motivates you to reach your best potential
Love
Love is love

No more clenching
No more shaking
No more overthinking
No more games
Entire body,
All at peace
Finally, I knew what love actually meant
Thank you for everything;
Here's to eternity
     I love you always

Balance is beauty
To be able to live a life you love
To be working towards your goals
And to be able to find someone who supports your every goal and dream alongside your own development
Is
love

From Ours to Yours- Eleni Sophia & pn.writes

24.01.19 the day our journeys intertwined
29.03.19 The day our lives changed incessantly

I had always dreamt of being with someone who supports all my dreams and goals
Little did I know
All these dreams and desires required patience and a dose of self-love
So, I could attract someone I had always wanted
Be patient beautiful intelligent girl
Everything is coming together for you

And when we stood under the full-moon moonlight
I felt nothing but true love and deep connection;
The moonlight charging us with its radiance and divinity-
With my hands encapsulated within yours
I had never felt so electrified
Connection between the universe
You And I
I realized we had our individual purposes in life, but they were forever significantly stronger when we are together

And for all those nights I stayed up and I couldn't sleep
When you took deep breaths with me-
Thank you for staying up with me
As I could hear your every breath
I just knew everything would be okay
Thank you for everything

And with each gaze
I fall in love all over again
Whatever you want from this world
Chase it
Engulf yourself fully in it
There was a point in our friendship we questioned 'distancing ourselves' for our own peace
We never wanted to hurt each other;
we forever wanted to be in each other's lives
Interfaith and long-distance? How could we?
But oh, my goodness, thank God we didn't give up before it even started
We trusted and look at us now
Stronger than ever- individually and together
Nobody can stop us- no distance can get in the way
Please, do not let anybody get in the way of your happiness
This life is too precious not to take chances
After all,
We only regret the chances we do not take

From Ours to Yours- Eleni Sophia & pn.writes

It's like I always knew something beautiful would evolve
out of this relationship
My subconscious just knew
You know when you just know
Yeah, that's the exact feeling I would feel
When we were just friends

I remember when we were just friends
I would tell you nobody in this world deserved you
What a privilege it is to be your first
I cannot wait to show you how incredibly beautiful love is

Great women will have you looking at life with such a beautiful perspective
A perspective you never even knew you had

From Ours to Yours- Eleni Sophia & pn.writes

You lose yourself
You find yourself
You heal
Engulf yourself within self-love
And the one you deserve finds you
Have faith sweetheart
Just have faith

Love has no race, religion or gender
Love is pure in all its forms
When two people from different backgrounds come together, accept one another for who they truly are, ignite with this non-judgmental attitude
Beautiful things begin;
We are children of the universe-
We are made of nothing but the same magical stardust;
Whether we are black, white, brown, blue-
We are love
No matter our gender, our religion
If two people have a desire to ignite their love and appreciation for one another
Absolutely nothing should get in the way-
The universe loves us and is forever smiling upon us all
It wants us to fight against these 'ideas' and fight for what we love
It wants us to put our trust in it and believe we can have the life we desire-
We took the chance and boy, do we have a ride ahead
But here we are- sharing our love with the world
Please, take your chance;
We hope nothing but the best for you
Good luck x

I hate the distance, but I know it will be worth every moment; we have such an amazing future ahead of us my King and I cannot wait to build this empire with you

You ask yourself, 'why wasn't I good enough', 'what was wrong with me?' but, oh my, you have no idea how much you will be for the right one. If you can love so truly and deeply, with so much purity and give so much love to the wrong one-
Just take a moment to think of how much the right one will appreciate you
Wait until you see what God was preparing you for

The whole time
He was working in the background
Putting obstacles in your way
To help you grow and evolve into the incredible woman you are
So, you can find, heal and love yourself
And then finally give the love you have always wanted to give
To the one who deserves you the most

Let us bring back the old-school kind of love
The love that does not leave you alone when you need it
the most-
The love that breaks boundaries
The love that never leaves you fighting alone
The love that does not give up on you
The one that goes against all odds
Just to be with you

Three years ago
I would never have imagined writing a letter of appreciation for the man who treats me the way I deserve
Thank you, God, for obstacles, growth and self-love
And most importantly,
Thank you
For him

From Ours to Yours- Eleni Sophia & pn.writes

All relationships have their hurdles
But when you keep God/the universe in the center
Everything will be okay
Surrender and let the starts above guide you both

And until our very last breath
It will always be you and me
Every moment I spend with you is a cherished moment
Every second I stare at you I realize I need nothing more from this world
The depth of your love
Insanely intensely Beautiful
The purity of our love- it is just everything about our love- unexplainable.
When I'm with you
Everything stops
The world around me pauses
As long as I have you by my side
I have everything I have ever needed

The hands of the universe are protecting you
You are being divinely held within the hands of the universe
Trust that the man God has for you will find you when you are ready to receive his love

The magical vibration of our intimacy
It is a whole other world when I'm in your presence
His soul is made of galaxies and
Hers is encapsulated with stars and stardust
Together they shine their light upon earth
To encourage and motivate
And to spread nothing but love

Be so complete that when this love arrives
You are so deeply connected within yourself and your cup is so full that you are actually able to pour and give
But also make sure you are getting the exact love you deserve
Remember to always have your cup filled first

And when our divine masculinity and femininity unite-
everything is so incredibly peaceful
I forget everything; when I am in this world with you- our
own little world- everything connects; individually, our
minds carry such beautiful perspectives,
But oh my, when they fuse and come together-
The energy is simply unexplainable

My handsome,
Loving you is the easiest thing I have ever done
Thank you for joining me on this journey
I cannot wait to be with you in this life
And for all those to come
This is the old-school love we have forever craved
We witnessed it growing up and it is something we both
wanted
We knew it was hard to find yet we had faith
After all,
At the end of it all,
We get what we deserve
And we deserve each other-
In this life, the next life and all those hereafter
You and me
Against all worlds

And maybe there is more than one love waiting for you at the door
Just remember to choose the one who deserves you
The one who satisfies your soul
Please do not choose somebody out of loneliness
Choose the one who you deserve
And the one deserving of your love

The magic you brought out in me
Sparkled into my life- enlightened me more than I could have imagined and made me realize anything before this was simply just a lesson

You made me realize how easy I am to love
And to have that thought changed in my mind-
Made everything else flow so magnificently

Thank you for reminding me daily how much I deserve
Thank you for doing everything in your power to see a smile on my face
Thank you for all your efforts
And most importantly,
Thank you for being you x

We so often get caught into the same mindsets of this generation
Let us bring back the chivalrous love
The one that makes you feel appreciated in their presence
The one that speaks to your soul
The one who understands the difference between just infatuation- (for this is not love)
and integrity- (the fundamental core of it all)

The purest and truest love ignites when
The strength between your partner and yourself is so intense
You're both helping each other grow
You're feeding each other's' minds
The love where you are exchanging, growing and evolving
And not just merely existing

The intensity between you two is one full of nothing but magic
That's the love we all crave for

From Ours to Yours- Eleni Sophia & pn.writes

The universe conspires to give you everything at exactly the right time
Love will find you when you are deeply ready within
The kind of love worth losing everything else for
Encapsulated yet liberated
Love so wholesome
Gratefulness and magic are what keep it thriving

Recreating our childhood memories
Going to the zoo, the museum
Exploring
Learning

It is not about how expensive the date
Or where you go
It's all about what you make of it
The maturity of our relationship is what makes it so special

And even when we are stuck in a long queue
We make the most out of the time we have together;
Playing silly games or appreciating one another in the moment
I cannot reiterate enough;
As long as I have him
I have everything

PN.WRITES

From Ours to Yours- Eleni Sophia & pn.writes

The magic in the path that lead me to you is ours paths
may have crossed a hundred times before
Just twisted around each other,
Isn't it funny how life managed to untangle it for us?

From Ours to Yours- Eleni Sophia & pn.writes

My heart was racing whenever I thought of her,
She made me feel so much at once,
I didn't know how to explain what had happened to me,
Everything hit me at once,
And yet to this day when I am with her, all I feel is peace, both hers and mine

Something clicked,
I knew it and felt it, her warm touch both inside and out,
Her perfection radiated throughout her whole body
Her kindness, her glow, invaded by body, it brightened up my soul

She is powerful and yet so gentle
The power injects you, her energy, it lifts you further than you have gone before,
Protect her heart,
The inner strength of mine comes through hers

From Ours to Yours- Eleni Sophia & pn.writes

I wasn't looking for you, and yet you found me
I wasn't seeking your love, and yet somehow it found me
Since the day we met, learning more about you, I found out so much more about me
Thank you for showing me love, thank you for showing me true peace

The spark in her eyes
You feel the energy she brings
Never resist it, embrace her power and channel it
She's electrifying and she is the source you have always looked for

Keep her lamp burning
She keeps the shadows away
The warmth she brings, you forget about the coldest of days
Be the reason that light never fades
Love her, cherish her, support her and most importantly, never let her forget what she means to you

Running my hands through her hair, I felt her peace
I felt at home, it didn't matter where we were, as long as she was by my side
No task was too great
No feat unachievable
I know if I ever get lost, if I have her, I am exactly where I'm meant to be

The four hours that feel like twenty minutes,
In precious minutes make her feel,
Feel love, feel happiness, feel protected
Knowing that this time you have with her,
Is time that no other can make you feel,
Time that drips away as you sit and hold each other,
The time you never want to end, and that time never has to,
But make sure she knows that that time would not want to be spent with anyone else except her

I want to stop time just so I can stare into her eyes a little longer, appreciate everything she does for me, Say thank you for giving me the world and the stars and more.

In her silence
You stop and stare at her
Admire her for her beauty
Grateful for her love
Knowing this bond could not be broken

In her silence
Her smile is enough to realize
That no other smile can bring you the same kind of joy
Each line cheek to cheek perfect in every curve, flawless
Always be the reason for that smile
Keep loving just as you do now, that smile will remain forever

In her silence,
As you embrace her
Feel her breathing
You feel peace, she is peace
And kindness and warmth
You feel at home because you are home
She is home, love throughout, love her forever

Just live and love her
Why worry about losing her
When you can spend the time loving her
Love her through all of it, the ups and downs,
She holds the key to your heart
Like no other could

flow is unmatched,
A melody so unique,
Only you and no one else could compose,
I stare in awe and amazement as you work,
And all I think is thank goodness I'm the man you chose to have by your side

And when I looked in her eyes
The starts shined so brightly
For in the moment he knew looking at her, she knew looking at him,
That the sparkle would only appear in each other's eyes and no one else's

Her eyes sat close to the moon
They peered out at the earth and looked at all she had given him
This world she created,
Everything she had ever given, wanted to give and will give was there for him
He was so excited to explore with her by his side, this world, and all of them

The gravity I felt towards her,
Her pull brought me so close
Stronger than the sun pulling the earth,
Jupiter himself would be in awe,
For her strength,
Is stronger than any planet, any god
Just as the planets orbit the sun
She is my star, my light and warmth,
An orbit I could never fall out of

From Ours to Yours- Eleni Sophia & pn.writes

When I see her in pain
I start to cry
For her pain is shared with mine
Her troubles are mine
We are a team and we are strong
She is my support I am hers,
For the world is hers and I want to be the one to give her it all

She created it,
It grew inside me and keeps growing,
Learning, and yet can never be perfect, her soul is too precious, so unmatched,
A soul from another world,
All I want to do is give her everything my world can

From Ours to Yours- Eleni Sophia & pn.writes

Time spent worrying about losing them
Is time wasted not loving them
The ups are amazing, the downs are inevitable,
But never give up on this love,
This love that comes once in a lifetime,
Make it the lifetime neither of you want to end

My Brave girl,
You allowed me into your life,
The brave girl who needs no support,
A woman who goes into the world and faces new challenges every day,
A woman who looks at a task, analyses it and attacks it,
Leaving the world in awe, about how one woman could command so much power, yet be so gentle and kind

From Ours to Yours- Eleni Sophia & pn.writes

A lot in this world is temporary
But she is forever
Love her, this life, the next and all the others
Love with everything, and when you have given everything, give some more
She pushes you to be better, you become greater,
She is your motivation and peace, your biggest fan
Appreciate every moment, both big and small, and love

They started as two separate entities
But as their energies combined
He felt her power
She felt his peace
Always, together stronger forever

Her glow was always there,
Somehow, she saw mine, she showed me there is more to me than I thought
She helps me grow day by day, she supports me in ways I never thought I would need,
She has given me a sense of home without having to be there, the warmth, the kindness,
I never imagined I would ever need what she has given me and now I can't imagine my life without her

Before I met her, I was a glass half full kind of person,
She showed me that it was more than about having it half full,
She taught me to fill it to the brim, and once it is full overflow it,
This woman is the forever girl, the shoulder for me to lean on, and the force spurring me on each day

We have a bond, never broken,
I sense her and she senses me,
It works in magical ways,
Our two-way direct link, where I can think as she is and she knows my response before I say it,
That bond is paranormal, I have found that one who senses me not in this life, but every life I have lived,
I found the person I am forever connected to

The world designed her to be more than what it could offer,
A jigsaw so complex the pieces are still being made,
As she lives her story the puzzle is completed a little more,
And yet it is never complete as she is the woman, the woman that changes everything,
The woman that can have no complete puzzle as each day she proves to the world as to why she is more than it can give, more than what is given to her

I was born to be different,
And found someone weirder,
Someone stranger,
Drove my curiosity,
A love so unique,
The only home where a world like ours could exist is our own

Some people make songs,
Some write poems,
I just want to express,
Express my ever-growing love for you
That grows day by day, minute by minute

From Ours to Yours- Eleni Sophia & pn.writes

The sun shone brighter on my world the day you came into it,
This love lives, it grows and evolves,
Each tree a new memory, every river an experience,
I simply lay and think,
I can't wait to populate our beautiful world

From Ours to Yours - Eleni Sophia & pn.writes

Hold her hand,
Forever a team,
She guides me, I guide her,
We take turns, we push each other to be at our strongest,
We support and we motivate,
The best of me comes through the best of her,
The energy combined becomes unstoppable,
unbreakable, and unmatched

For you,
My love, it is for you,
A world we are building, everything I build for you,
The walls that will build our home,
My heart and soul,
For the love you have given me opened my life up, and for that, everything of mine, everything you have given me, it's all for you

From Ours to Yours- Eleni Sophia & pn.writes

I tried to draw a life in the stars,
Where all my dreams achieved,
A life full of happiness,
But this drawing was never complete before you,
without the queen in my kingdom, the empire means nothing

One reason why this works so well is because before our journeys intertwined, our cups were full of endless self-love

All relationships have disagreements and arguments but it's about how you overcome these challenges together

Close your eyes and leap,
You have chosen a life with me,
We took the leap of faith,
Any challenge we work together,
The most amazing part of the adventure is that it is not the destination that ever matters, it's that I'm with you every step of the way as we take it

We stayed up and talked,
So long that the stars went to sleep, and the sun woke up,
And yet even after speaking to her for so long, there was so much more to say, so much more to do,
To this day, I'm still learning and that's the beauty of what we have and I hope you have, every time I speak to her, she makes me laugh, makes me smile and makes me feel grateful for being able to know she is only a call away

I crave to hear your voice,
That frequency the waves of my love live on,
It is just that something in your voice,
I hear it and it lifts me

It is a relationship where there is never and will be a goodbye, it's a goodnight and see you tomorrow

I live for the moments,
Where all the lights are lit,
And yet I look in her eyes and they are brighter than any I can see,
For she shines, brighter than the sun, than the stars and I am so lucky,
That I'm the one she allows to see into her mind

From Ours to Yours- Eleni Sophia & pn.writes

Our heart beats were in in sync, hers and mine,
They formed the rhythm our song,
A song only we knew, a song so melodic we felt it,
In heart and soul this tune was ours, and no one else's

From Ours to Yours- Eleni Sophia & pn.writes

We are young,
We are in love,
We don't know what the world is going to throw at us, a lifetime of dreams achieved, challenges faced, experiences sought and given to us,
Yet we both know that we don't want anyone else to experience them other than each other

We live in a world where we can be connected to
another person in a mere matter of seconds,
Yet no connection can match this,
No words need to be uttered,
This connection doesn't come through words, doesn't
come through action
It comes through feeling

She asked me how she looked tonight,
'My love, you look beautiful tonight, just like you do every night, every day and always,
You are beautiful because your soul was made that way and the way you live your life extends that beauty,'
Her heart is pure and beautiful, I just want to protect it always

This growth mindset we share,
Allows us to think as individuals, to live our own lives,
It's amazing how we go about the same goals, but we have different approaches,
We make our own noise, the world listens to us,
What bonds us is the love we share for everything we do, as individuals and together

The longer I see you,
The harder it is to say goodbye,
We get a glimpse of our life together and yet our lives as individuals pull us apart,
But no matter where in time or space I am, you are on my mind
All day every day, for that dream life together is coming,
In its own time silently waiting for the day that we fully become one

To the love forever waiting,
The love so far away I yearn for the day,
The day when I get to come home to it,
Get to hold it so tight grasp that love in my hand and say it is mine,
You might be so far away from me now, but I promise,
Our worlds are doing all they can so that they join to become one,
Just like the explosion that started this world,
Our worlds will collide and that love that is so far away,
will be intertwined in our daily life together,
It shall grow more than it has done, for this love, this inevitable everlasting love, is where the print of my soul shall forever last
This heart will never stop beating for as long as she is here,
She gives me life, and a life worth living,
The purpose of my heart is to make sure hers never suffers

When our minds resonate,
Our heads race with wild thoughts and images of yesterday, our life tomorrow,
Racing so that reality can never catch us, for where we are heading, our dream world is becoming a reality,
A reality only the two of us belong in, for the rest of the world will never understand,
The reality we are creating is more than what already and could ever exist

We are a little different
We share values, morals, beliefs,
And yet all I crave is to get to know her more,
Her family, her culture,
The more I understand where she comes from and she I, the more we evolve mindsets,
The more I understand about her faith, the more ours grows together

I close my eyes and you are there,
Your beautiful soul, I see it I embrace it,
I close my eyes, I hear your voice,
That soft gentle tone, it warms me inside out,
I close my eyes, I feel your touch,
Your love lies in my heart, locked away so no other can take it

The background doesn't matter
It's never a difference
It's an opportunity for you to learn, to grown
Another language another tradition, the clothes she wears, the food she eats,
You meet, you diversify the earth, we unite, and we learn,
Never finish learning, about others, about her, and most importantly about yourself,
We are never the same people throughout our whole life, so give her the best of you and be the best you can for her, she is worth every minute

We were born different, but we think the same,
Were raised different, yet similar values,
Lived such different lives, that now somehow complement each other,
No one else dictates the relationship, it works for us and it is beautiful

Her eyes lit up so bright,
the shooting stars racing across the sky stopped dead in the night,
to witness what it was like to see a phenomenon out of their world

A message from the writers

Thank you so much for all your incredible support! Thank you for taking your time to read through our words, thank you for choosing us and thank you for all your support on our social media!

We hope you enjoyed reading 'From Ours to Yours;' we wrote this from our love, to your love! We hope you found our words relatable and completed your journey through our poetry with a fresh perspective!

What is yours will never pass you. You are on this incredible journey of life with everything working in your favor. We hope you find love within yourself; we hope you find the love you deserve and most importantly, we wish you nothing but endless happiness and love.

Please never stop fighting for what you love- no matter what the circumstance; take the leap of faith; you never know the outcome if you don't try.

We are proud and so blessed to have crossed paths and we are so incredibly grateful to be in a relationship where our love gets stronger as each day passes. Long-Distance and Interfaith can get hard, but, with the right person by your side, a dose of faith and an optimistic mindset, anything is achievable.

Not being able to see each other daily hurts- a lot on some days- but knowing we are trying to make the world a better place together- even whilst being so far away, eases things a little.

From Ours to Yours- Eleni Sophia & pn.writes

Time is a phenomenon,
Time to heal, time to change, time to grow,
It is not one thing, it is how we choose to define it,
Time is the one thing everchanging and everything changes with it,
My life changed the day I met you,
You sprouted a newfound feeling within me,
And as time has continued to pass, this feeling has grown,
You've allowed me to feel, both inside and out,
This time, it has allowed me to grow as a person,
Its taught me how to be vulnerable, how to allow someone into my life and learn about someone else's,
The complexities every single human faces from so many perspectives, it amazes me how you juggle everything in your life, you leave me in awe,
In awe of how you can live your life and yet give your man the time and patience to listen to him and how his day was, you give me your time,
Time - the one thing in life you can never take back, and you give that to me, my gratitude has no bounds my love

We appreciate you so much and would once again like to thank you for coming on this journey.

If you would like to see more from us, please feel free to follow our Instagram pages where we post more of our writings:

@eleniisophia & @pn.writes

Thank you!

This is

From Ours to Yours

Lots of love

Eleni Sophia & pn.writes
xx

Also by Eleni Sophia & pn.writes:
Everythinglongdistance.org
where you can find their Rose Quartz shop: Eunoia- charged homeware crystal diffusers- perfect for those in long-distance relationships!

Copyright © 2020 Eleni Sophia & pn.writes

'From Ours to Yours'

Perspective Press Global Ltd

All rights reserved.

ISBN: 978-1-8380044-4-6

www.ingramcontent.com/pod-product-compliance
Lightning Source LLC
Chambersburg PA
CBHW021442080526
44588CB00009B/650